The Mighty Work of God

SELF GOVERNMENT

A Child's History of the United States of America

By Ruth J. Smith

Illustrated by Lisa M. Mikler

First Edition
Copyright © 2002, by Ruth J. Smith

Published by
Bradford Press
South Bend, Indiana

All rights reserved. No part of this work may be reproduced in any form without permission in writing from the author.

All Scripture quotations are taken from the King James Version of the Bible.

Printed by The C. J. Krehbiel Company
Cincinnati, Ohio

Graphic Design by DOV Graphics
Cincinnati, Ohio

Library of Congress Catalog Number 2002093374
ISBN 0-9705618-1-4

Cover Art and Illustrations by Lisa M. Mikler. Maps by Mountain High Maps ® Copyright © 1993 Digital Wisdom, Inc. *John Wyclif*, engraving by H. M. Paget in Harper's Magazine, 1888, Mary Evans Picture Library, London. *John 1* from the Tyndale Bible, The British Library, St. John Title Page, Shelfmark c.188.a.17 *The New Testament*, William Tyndale, 1526. *John Smith*, unidentified artist, National Portrait Gallery, Smithsonian Institution. *Pocahontas*, unidentified artist, after the 1616 engraving by Simone Van De Passe, National Portrait Gallery, Smithsonian Institution; gift of the A.W. Mellon Educational and Charitable Trust, 1942. *Virginia/ Discovered described by Captain John Smith*, 1606, Library of Congress. *Alexander Graham Bell's Design Sketch of the Telephone*, ca 1876. Library of Congress. *Reproduced by Permission.*

Dedication

*To the Grandchildren God has
given me and
to the Boys and Girls of
the 21st Century in America
that they might remember
the mighty works of God
in bringing forth this nation
and not forget His works.*

Table of Contents

1. His Story 1
2. Government 3
3. Civil Government 7
4. God's Providence 9
5. In the Beginning 13
6. God Created the Continents 17
7. God Created Man 23
8. Moses and the Law 27
9. Christ Changed History 33
10. Apostle Paul: *Link to Europe* 37
11. A Bible for the People 41
12. Christopher Columbus: *Link to the New World* 51
13. The Earliest Settlement: *Jamestown* 73
14. The Pilgrims: *Seed of our Christian Republic* 81
15. One Nation Under God 97

v

16. George Washington: *Father of
    Our Country* 99
17. Daniel Boone: *God's Man for
    Opening the Western Frontier* 109
18. Keeping One Nation Under God 119
19. Abraham Lincoln 121
20. Communication across a Nation 133
21. The Nation Expands 149

Chapter 1
His Story

That they might set their hope in God, and not forget the works of God. Psalm 78:7

History? What is history?

Why do we study history? Many people do not know why they should study history. This book will help each student to learn why we should study history and how important history is.

Ever since God created the earth, He has been working in it. History tells all that God has done in the lives of men and nations. So we can say that history is *His Story* or God's story.

The Bible says that we should remember what God has done. We should remember how God has worked since the very beginning of time. The more we learn about all that God has done, the more we will learn to love God.

Studying history will help us see how God works in the life of each person — man, woman, boy or girl. Studying history will also show us how God gave us our nation — the United States of America.

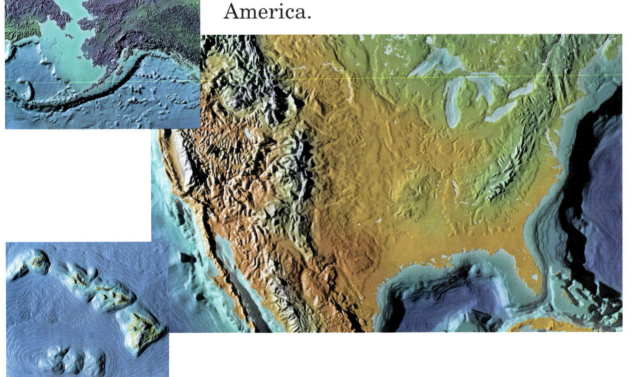

Chapter 2
Government

*For as he thinketh in his heart,
so is he. Proverbs 23:7a*

When Noah Webster wrote his 1828 *Dictionary*, he said that government means "direction" and "control".

Each person is governed — directed or controlled — by something. Each man, woman or child makes many decisions every day. We decide what to say, what to wear, what to eat, and how to act.

> A good man out of the good treasure of the heart bringeth forth good things: and an evil man out of the evil treasure bringeth forth evil things.

The Bible tells us that the ideas and thoughts which are in our heart will decide how we act. If our thoughts and ideas are controlled by the Bible, then our actions will also be controlled by the Bible. If our thoughts and ideas are not controlled by the

Bible, then our actions will not be controlled by the Bible.

In Matthew 12:35, the Bible reminds us: "A good man out of the good treasure of the heart bringeth forth good things: and an evil man out of the evil treasure bringeth forth evil things."

Keeping the heart true to good things is not easy. Louisa May Alcott wrote about the hard task of governing the heart in her poem, *My Kingdom*.

My Kingdom
by Louisa May Alcott

A little kingdom I possess
Where thoughts and feelings dwell,
And very hard I find the task
Of governing it well;
For passion tempts and troubles me,
A wayward will misleads,
And selfishness its shadow casts
On all my words and deeds.

Government

How can I learn to rule myself,
To be the child I should,
Honest and brave, nor ever tire
Of trying to be good?
How can I keep a sunny soul
To shine along life's way?
How can I tune my little heart
To sweetly sing all day?

Dear Father, help me with the love
That casteth out my fear;
Teach me to lean on thee,
and feel
That thou art very near,
That no temptation
is unseen,
No childish grief too small,
Since thou,
with patience infinite,
Doth soothe and
comfort all.

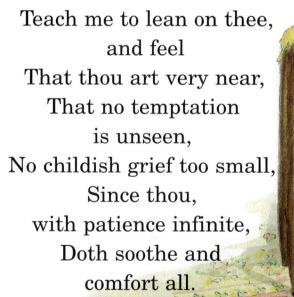

> I do not ask for any crown
> But that which all may win,
> Nor seek to conquer any world,
> Except the one within.
> Be thou my guide until I find,
> Led by a tender hand,
> Thy happy kingdom in *myself,*
> And dare to take command.

God's Word teaches us how to govern our own hearts.

When we choose to say and do the things God tells us to do in His Word, we direct and control ourselves. This is self government.

God has also given us our parents, pastors and teachers who help to govern us. They do this by making rules and laws in our home, our church, and our classroom.

We must remember, the best way to be governed is to direct our own actions the way God tells us to in His Word.

Chapter 3
Civil Government

God knew that families would live together in cities and nations. They would need a way to protect each person. They must protect each person's property.

God has a plan for civil government. Civil government controls and directs men in cities and nations. Civil government makes laws to protect each person's life and property.

God planned for the laws to be based upon the Bible. If each person controls his actions according to the Bible, he will need less civil government. If he does not control his own actions, he will need more civil government.

Men did not always have the Bible. They

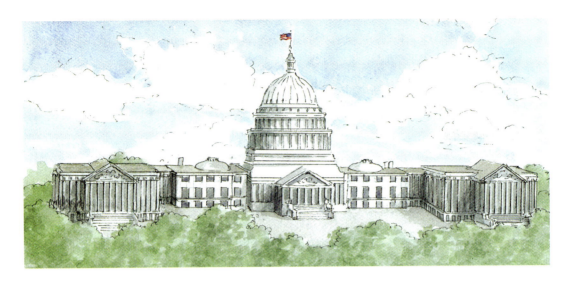

did not know what God had planned for civil government. They thought that the king could control men any way he pleased. This was not a Christian idea.

God's plan is for the people to direct or control their own civil government. They should choose the ones who would rule over them.

In the United States of America, we choose the men or women who will direct our city, state or nation. It is important for us to learn what the Bible teaches about civil government. Then we can choose the right people for the job of civil government.

Chapter 4
God's Providence

The Bible teaches us that God cares for all of His creatures — this care is God's Providence.

He cares for the fish of the sea. He cares for the birds in the air. He cares for each of the animals on the earth, both big and small. He even cares for the plants. But most of all, He cares for each man, woman, boy and girl.

The Bible says: "Are not two sparrows sold for a farthing? and one of them shall not fall on the ground without your Father. But the

> God cares for all of His creatures — this is God's Providence

very hairs of your head are all numbered. Fear ye not therefore, ye are of more value than many sparrows." Matthew 10:29-31.

"Sing unto the Lord with thanksgiving;. . .Who covereth the heaven with clouds, who prepareth rain for the earth, who maketh grass to grow upon the mountains. He giveth to the beast his food, and to the young ravens which cry." Psalm 147:7-9.

God's Care and Protection are Seen in History

History tells us about God's care of men, women, boys, and girls. God protected and cared for them, when they could not.

Feeding of the Five Thousand

"And when it was evening, his disciples came to him, saying, This is a desert place, and the time is now past; send the multitude away, that they may go into the villages, and buy themselves victuals.

"But Jesus said unto them, They need not depart; give ye them to eat.

"And they say unto him, We have here but five loaves, and two fishes.

"He said, Bring them hither to me. And he commanded the multitude to sit down on the grass, and took the five loaves, and the two fishes, and looking up to heaven, he blessed, and brake, and gave the loaves to his disciples, and the disciples to the multitude. And they did all eat, and were filled: and they took up of the fragments that remained twelve baskets full. And they that had eaten were about five thousand men, beside women and children." Matthew 14:15-21.

The Pilgrims Find a New Home and a Friend

When the Pilgrims arrived in America, they did not arrive at the place where they had planned. No one was there to welcome them. But God cared for them.

The first winter was very difficult. Over half of the settlers died during that winter.

The Pilgrims knew there were Indians that lived in the area. They did not know how the Indians would treat them. Many times, they saw Indians in the trees. When they tried to talk with them, the Indians ran away. One time, while the Pilgrims were eating their dinner, the Indians stole some of the Pilgrims' tools.

In March, an Indian walked right into their village and spoke to them in English. He didn't speak very well, but they could understand what he said. His name was Samoset.

He told them about another Indian who had been in England and could speak better English. His name was Squanto.

Squanto became a friend to the Pilgrims. He helped them plant their corn. He taught them how to catch fish and trap game. He also helped them talk to the other Indians. The Pilgrims were able to trade with the Indians and to live at peace with them.

God cared for the Pilgrims by giving them a special friend, Squanto.

Chapter 5
In the Beginning

*In the beginning God created
the heaven and the earth.
Genesis 1:1*

History began with creation. Time began with creation.

God created the earth. He made it from nothing. In just six days, He created everything. Think of all the things that God made.

Creation teaches us many things about God. Only God could fill the earth with so many wonderful things. Only God could create so much variety.

If you study the plants, there are very many kinds of plants. Each plant is different and special.

If you study the birds, there are very many kinds of birds. Each bird is different and special.

If you study the fish, there are very many kinds of fish. Each fish is different and very special.

If you study the animals, there are very many kinds of animals. Each animal is different and special.

God made many different creatures on the earth.

God also made everything very beautiful.

When we look at the beautiful sky, we know that God must be beautiful. When we look at the tall mountains, again we know that God is a God of beauty.

Creation also teaches us that God is very powerful. The wind, the waves, and the weather all obey God.

Chapter 6

God Created the Continents

On the third day of creation, God formed the dry land and the seas. God made seven great bodies of land — these are called continents. A continent is land with water almost all of the way around it.

Each continent has its own shape. God made each continent for a special reason.

Asia

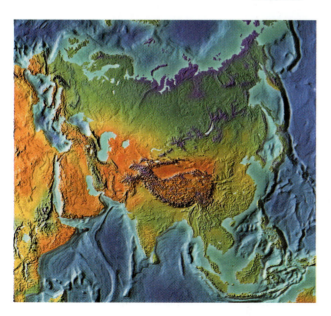

Asia is the largest continent. Asia is close to all of the other continents. Asia has the highest mountains of any continent.

God placed the first people on the continent of Asia.

When Christ came to earth, He came to the continent of Asia. God made Asia to be the continent of beginnings.

Europe

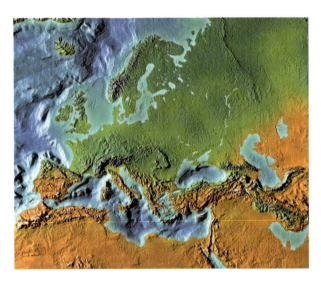

Europe is quite different from Asia. The weather in Europe is more mild. The mountains are not as high. Europe has more coast line than any other continent.

It was not as hard to travel around Europe as it was in Asia. It was easier for people to share ideas in Europe.

God used Paul to teach about Jesus in Europe. Many people in Europe became Christians. God helped some men in Europe to understand the ideas of government found in the Bible. These ideas helped form the United States of America.

North America

North America is very different from Europe and Asia. North America is far from the continents of Europe and Asia. The Atlantic Ocean is on the east. The Pacific Ocean is on the west. North America was not settled until God 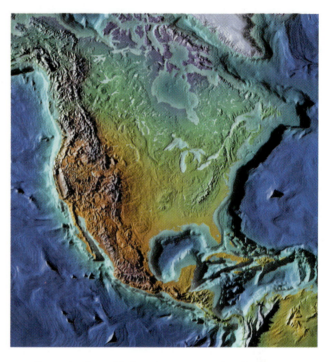 had the right people ready to build a new nation.

The United States of America was set up as one nation under God. Its laws were based upon the Bible. Each person had more liberty than ever before in history.

God made pairs of continents. Each continent in the north has a partner in the south.

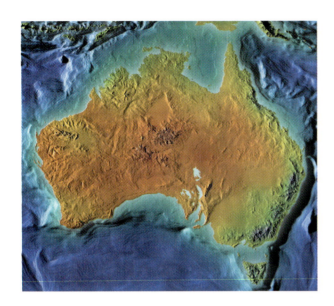

Australia

Australia is the partner to the continent of Asia. Australia has many rare plants and animals.

Africa

Africa is the partner to the continent of Europe. Africa has the grandest kinds of animals.

South America

South America is the partner to North America. South America has the most beautiful plants of all of the continents.

Antarctica

Antarctica is the continent at the south pole. It is covered with ice. God's plan for Antarctica is to help control the climate of the globe. Someday we may learn more about God's plan for Antarctica.

Chapter 7
God Created Man

> God created man in his own image, in the image of God created he him.

On the sixth day of creation, God created man. Man was made in the image of God.

Man was made to live forever. God gave man a soul. No other creature has a soul. A cat does not have a soul. A dog does not have a soul. They will not live forever. God only created man with a soul and to live forever.

God made man more like Himself than any other creature. God did not make man like

the animals He had created. God's nature is shown in each man, woman, boy and girl.

God made each part of His creation unique. So God also made each person unique. Each one is different from any other person. Each man, woman, boy and girl shows the great variety of God's creation.

Man was made to glorify God. "I have created him for my glory, I have formed him; yea, I have made him." Isaiah 43:7. "Thou art worthy, O Lord, to receive glory and honour and power: for thou hast created all things, and for thy pleasure they are and were created." Revelation 4:11.

God Created Man 25

All of God's creation belongs to Him because He is the Creator. Each man, woman, boy and girl belongs to God. God is the one who gives each person life and breath. He chooses how long each person should live.

God has a purpose for each person which He created. God uses men, women, boys, and girls to do His work on the earth.

Part of man's work is to care for the earth. God told him to "have dominion over the fish of the sea, and over the fowl of the air, and over every living thing that moveth upon the earth." Genesis 1:28.

God made the plants and the trees to feed man and animals.

The laws of God, in the Bible, tell man how to use all that God has created.

Sin Changed Man's Walk with God

Adam and Eve were the first man and woman created by God. Adam and Eve chose to disobey God. Disobeying God is sin.

In the Garden of Eden, Adam and Eve could walk  and talk with God. When Adam and Eve sinned, God moved them out of the Garden of Eden. Adam and Eve now had sin in their hearts. They could not walk and talk with God. God had to control and direct them with His laws.

Chapter 8
Moses and the Law

When Moses was born, his family lived in Egypt. They were part of the people known as the Israelites or the Children of Israel. They had lived in Egypt for many years.

Egypt had a king called Pharaoh. Pharaoh made the laws, because he was the king. The laws he made did not please God.

The king made the Children of Israel his slaves. He gave them many hard tasks.

Many babies were born to the Israelites. The king thought that there were too many Israelites. He was afraid they would become his enemy. He wanted to kill all of their baby boys.

God Cared for Moses

Moses's mother knew that the king's law said that all baby boys should be killed. God led her to hide Moses. She knew she could only hide him when he was very small.

When Moses was three months old, his mother made a little ark or basket for him out of bulrushes. She made it so that it would float on water. Moses's mother put Moses in the little basket and put it in the river.

God cared for Moses while he was in the basket. The king's daughter found him in the little basket.

"And when she had opened it, she saw the child: and, behold, the babe wept. And she had compassion on him, and said, This is one of the Hebrews' children." Exodus 2:6.

Pharaoh's daughter kept Moses as her own son. He lived in the palace. He was trained and taught as if he were the princess's son.

Moses used by God as Deliverer, Lawgiver, and Historian

Moses as Deliverer

God cared for Moses when he was a baby. God had a plan for Moses when he was a man.

The Children of Israel were very unhappy as slaves under Pharaoh. They cried unto God for help.

God told Moses to ask Pharaoh to let the Children of Israel leave Egypt. Moses did not think he could do that. But God said He would help Moses and teach him what to say. God also sent Aaron, Moses's brother, to help Moses.

Moses and Aaron went to see Pharaoh. They told Pharaoh that the God of Israel wanted Pharaoh to let the Children of Israel leave. "And Pharaoh said, Who is the Lord, that I should obey his voice to let Israel go? I know not the Lord, neither will I let Israel go." Exodus 5:2.

Pharaoh did not want to let the Children of Israel go. He was angry. He made their work harder and harder.

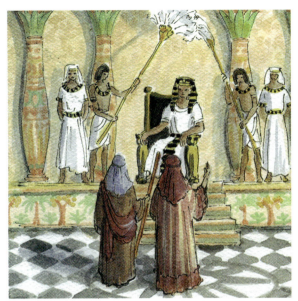

Pharaoh did not obey God. Pharaoh did not let the Children of Israel leave. God sent ten judgments to change Pharaoh's heart. God sent these judgments on Pharaoh and the people of Egypt.

At last, Pharaoh let the people go.

God used Moses to lead the Israelites out of Egypt. "And the Lord went before them by day in a pillar of a cloud, to lead them the way; and by night in a pillar of fire, to give them light; to go by day and night." Exodus 13:21.

Moses as Lawgiver

Since man is a sinner, he needs laws to direct his actions. God used Moses to give His laws to the people.

"And the LORD said unto Moses, Come up to me into the mount, and be there: and I will give thee

Moses and the Law 31

tables of stone, and a law, and commandments which I have written; that thou mayest teach them . . .

"And Moses went up into the mount, and a cloud covered the mount. And the glory of the LORD abode upon mount Sinai, and the cloud covered it six days: and the seventh day he called unto Moses out of the midst of the cloud. And the sight of the glory of the LORD was like devouring fire on the top of the mount in the eyes of the children of Israel. And Moses went into the midst of the cloud, and gat him up into the mount: and Moses was in the mount forty days and forty nights." Exodus 24:12-18.

God made laws to govern the people. He wrote the Law on tablets and gave it to Moses. Moses gave the Law to the people.

Moses as Historian

God planned for Moses to be the world's first historian. An historian writes down the events of God working in the lives of men and nations. Moses told how God worked from the time of creation through the end of Moses's life.

The books written by Moses are the first five books of the Bible: Genesis, Exodus, Leviticus, Numbers and Deuteronomy.

Chapter 9
Christ Changed History

Christ came to earth 4,000 years after creation. All the events of history before Christ made the way for His coming.

The Bible teaches that "When the fulness of the time was come, God sent forth his Son." Galatians 4:4a. God sent His Son, Jesus Christ, to the earth

> When the fulness of the time was come, God sent forth his Son.

when the world was ready for Him.

Jesus came to earth as a baby. Angels told the shepherds in the fields that Jesus was born. "And there were in the same country shepherds abiding in the field, keeping watch over their flock by night. And, lo, the angel of the Lord came upon them, and the glory of the Lord shone round about them: and they were sore afraid. And the angel said unto them, Fear not: for, behold, I bring you good tidings of great joy, which shall be to all people. For unto you is born this day in the city of David a Saviour, which is Christ the Lord." Luke 2:8-11.

God also sent a special star which led wise men from the east. The star led them to Bethlehem where Jesus was. "When they saw the star, they rejoiced with exceeding great joy. And when they were come into the house, they saw the young child with Mary

his mother, and fell down, and worshipped him." Matthew 2:10-11.

Jesus came to the earth to give salvation to each man, woman, boy or girl who trusts in Him. "For God so loved the world, that he gave his only begotten Son, that whosoever believeth in him should not perish, but have everlasting life." John 3:16.

Jesus had to die in our place for our sins. His blood had to be shed to give us salvation. Jesus died, but then He rose from the dead. He went back to Heaven to be with His Heavenly Father.

Salvation gives eternal life. Each man, woman, boy or girl who trusts in Jesus Christ will live forever with Jesus.

When a person accepts God's gift of salvation, the Holy Spirit comes to live in his heart. The Holy Spirit helps each person to direct and control himself by the Word of God.

Jesus's death on the cross made the way for each person to be governed in his heart. This is Christian self government.

The Word of God helps each person know what is right and wrong. It shows each person how to govern himself. As people lived by the Word of God and had Christian self government, it changed their lives. Others looked at them and could not understand why they acted the way they did.

Once people learned to govern themselves in their hearts, they began to govern their own families.

After hundreds of years, people had the Bible and understood that if they could govern their own families, they could also govern their own cities, states, and nations.

Each person had to be able to study the Bible for himself.

Chapter 10
Apostle Paul

Link to Europe

*And a vision appeared to Paul in the night;
There stood a man of Macedonia,
and prayed him, saying,
Come over into Macedonia, and help us.
Acts 16:9*

After Christ went back to heaven, God used other men to spread the good news of the Gospel in Asia. Churches were started in many cities.

Paul was an apostle of Jesus. Paul went to many of the churches of Asia. He taught and preached about Jesus.

The Bible tells us that Paul had a dream. In the dream, a man of Macedonia was calling him. The man asked Paul to come to help them. Macedonia was in Europe.

Paul knew the dream was from God. He was ready to go to Macedonia right away. He knew "that the Lord had called us for to preach the gospel unto them." Acts 16:10.

Paul was the first person to tell the people in Europe the good news about Jesus.

The book of Acts tells about the first Christian in Europe. She was a woman named Lydia. "And a certain woman named Lydia, a seller of purple, of the city of Thyatira, which worshipped God, heard us: whose heart the Lord opened, that she attended unto the things which were spoken of Paul." Acts 16:14.

Paul preached and taught the Gospel in many cities. The Gospel soon spread through all the continent of Europe.

God inspired Paul to write letters to churches where he preached. He also wrote letters to special Christian friends. Those letters became a part of the New Testament.

God used Paul to take the gospel to Europe. He  was the link for the Gospel to go from Asia to Europe.

Hundreds of years later, the first Bibles were printed in Europe for all the people to read.

Chapter 11
A Bible for the People

The writing of the Bible, God's Word, was finished by about 90 A.D. The first copies were written by hand on scrolls. The Old Testament was written in the Hebrew language. The New Testament was written in the Greek language.

At the time of Christ, the people in Asia and Europe spoke Greek. That is why the New Testament was written in Greek.

In New Testament times, there were many small churches. These churches governed themselves. There was a church at Jerusalem, a church at Antioch, a church at Ephesus. There were also churches in other cities. Many churches began in Europe because Paul preached and taught there.

By 1300 A.D., or 1300 years after the time of Christ, the churches had changed. Instead of small churches that governed themselves, most of the churches were governed by the church at Rome. The church at Rome had become very strong. It chose what should be taught in the other churches.

Since Latin was used by the church of Rome, the Bible was translated into Latin. Only the church leaders could read the Bible. The people could not have their own copy of the Bible or even look at the Bible.

When people cannot read the Bible for themselves, it is easy for them to follow wrong ideas and teachings. The church of Rome taught the people that there could only be one church. That church was the church of Rome.

John Wycliffe

God used John Wycliffe to help the people of England. He was born at Wickliffe, in England, about 1324. He studied at Oxford University. He became the pastor of a church in Lutterworth.

A Bible for the People

John Wycliffe knew that the Bible was the most important book of all. He wanted everyone to read it, not just the church leaders. The Roman Church did not want the people to have their own Bible.

The people of England were having hard times. John Wycliffe knew that the Bible had the answers the people needed. He knew that the Bible must be translated so that the people could read it for themselves. He wanted the English people to have God's Word in English rather than Latin.

By 1382, Wycliffe had finished translating the Latin Bible into English. There were no printing presses. Wycliffe's work was copied by hand. There were only a few copies of the whole English Bible, but many copies were made of some parts of the Scripture. Copies were made of single books from the Bible. These copies were given to people all over England.

The men who believed the teachings of John Wycliffe were called Lollards. They copied the Scriptures in small booklets or tracts. Then they went across England preaching and giving people God's Word. The people of England loved the Bible. They were very happy to have a Bible or even a part of the Bible for their very own.

Many people did not know how to read. The Lollards taught the people how to read, so they could read the Bible. The Bible was in English and they loved to read it for themselves. They wanted to learn the truths of the Bible.

Historians tell us that if you met two people on the road in England, at least one of the two would have followed the teachings of Wycliffe.

The Printing Press

In Wycliffe's time, copies of the Bible had to be written by hand. This took a very long time and only a few copies of the Bible could be made.

Johannes Gutenberg was born in 1410 and lived in Germany. God used him to invent a new kind of printing press. It could be used to print the Bible.

A Bible for the People

Before Gutenberg's printing press, the printer carved each page on a wooden block. The block was then covered with ink and stamped on the paper. It took a long time to carve each page and too long to print a book.

Gutenberg's printing press had movable type. Each letter was a separate block of wood. The printer put the letters in order to make the words and sentences.

Once the letters were in order in the wooden tray, the printer put ink on the letters. The tray with the letters was laid against a sheet of paper. Then the printer used the press to push the tray of letters against the paper. The printer took the printed page from the press and hung it on a line to dry.

The letter blocks could be used over and over. They were called movable type. It still took a long time, but whole books could more easily be printed.

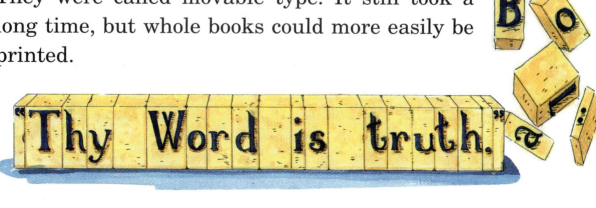

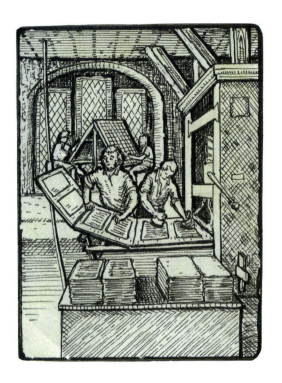

The Bible was the first important book to be printed on Gutenberg's printing press. The printing press helped many, many more people have the Bible to read.

The Roman church rulers did not want the people to read the Bible. Laws were made to keep the people from having the Bible.

William Tyndale

About 100 years after Gutenberg invented the printing press, William Tyndale was born in England. God used William Tyndale to be the father of our English Bible.

John Wycliffe had translated the Bible from Latin. William Tyndale was able to translate the Bible from the languages in which it was first written.

A Bible for the People

William Tyndale had studied the Word of God. He knew it was very important for each person to read the Bible for himself. He did not think the church leaders should be the only ones who could have a Bible. He declared, "If God preserves my life, I will cause a boy that driveth a plow to know more of the Scriptures than the pope."

The Roman Church and the laws of England kept the Bible away from the people. The leaders knew that if the people read the Bible, they would want to govern themselves and their own churches.

The King punished anyone who shared the Bible with others. Sometimes they were put in prison. Sometimes they died.

William Tyndale knew that God wanted him to translate the Bible. He left England and hid at other places in Europe.

The King of England had spies who told him where William Tyndale was. The spies told the King that Tyndale was translating the Bible.

The King sent soldiers, who put William Tyndale in prison. William Tyndale loved God and knew that the people must have the Word of God. Even while Tyndale was in prison, he kept working on the Bible.

Tyndale had a helper, John Rogers. When Tyndale was taken to prison, Rogers saved all Tyndale's work.

Rogers secretly printed Tyndale's Bible. Sometimes the King's soldiers found the hiding places and broke the printing presses.

Tyndale was pleased that Rogers had printed the Old Testament. Tyndale imagined how the Word of God would be sent from house to house and from city to city. This gave Tyndale joy even while he was in prison. He kept working to finish the translation of the whole Bible.

Everyone Tyndale met saw his love for God and for other people. Even his jailer liked to hear him talk about Jesus Christ.

A Bible for the People

The jailer brought his daughter and others from his house to see Tyndale. He wanted them to know about the Gospel, too. The jailer, his daughter, and others from his house became Christians.

William Tyndale had great peace in his heart. Although Tyndale was in prison, the Word of God was not.

On October 6, 1536, William Tyndale was put to death. Tyndale was calm, even though he knew he was going to die. The King had ordered his death. But Tyndale still prayed for him. William Tyndale's prayer before he died was for the King: "Lord, open the king of England's eyes!"

God used Tyndale's translation after his death. Within one year, Tyndale's translation of the Bible was brought to the King. The King looked at the Bible. Tyndale's name was not in it. A special page was written to honor the King. The King said the

Bible could be sold in England.

The people of England had been waiting for the Bible. Whoever had enough money bought the Bible and read it. Some asked others to read God's Word to them. Older people learned to read so they could read the Bible. In many places people met so they could learn to read. Families who did not have enough money to buy a Bible shared the cost with others. Then they met together and read it.

The Word of God began to work in the hearts and lives of the people in England.

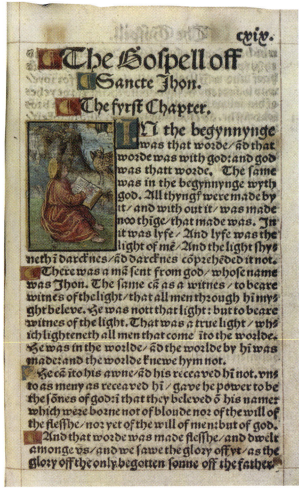

Chapter 12
Christopher Columbus

Link to the New World

In 1382, Wycliffe translated the Bible for the people of England. They loved to read the Bible and were learning how to govern themselves.

The people of England and Europe knew little about the world. They did not know how big it was.

They did not know about all of the continents.

A little more than 100 years after Wycliffe translated the Bible, God opened the door to the New World. He used Christopher Columbus.

A Boy with a Dream

The Columbus family lived in Genoa, Italy.

About 1450, a boy was born to the Columbus family. The boy was named Christopher.

The city of Genoa was a busy seaport. Many ships sailed in and out of Genoa. They carried goods from other parts of the world to trade with the merchants of Genoa.

As a boy, Christopher watched the ships sail to and from Genoa. He wanted to learn all about sailing.

Christopher's father and grandfather were cloth makers. Christopher did not want to be a cloth maker. He knew he wanted to sail in a ship someday.

Christopher learned to read and write. He studied arithmetic. He loved to learn about the earth. He read about the sun, moon, and stars. He also studied about sailing.

When he was only fourteen, Christopher sailed in a large ship for the first time.

To Portugal

By the time Columbus was twenty-five years old, he had made many trips on the Mediterranean Sea. He had visited many countries. On one voyage,

Columbus's ship sailed from the Mediterranean Sea into the great Western Ocean. The ship was sailing to England.

One day warships came near. Cannons were shot toward Columbus's ship. Columbus and the other sailors fought back. They shot their guns at the warships.

The fight lasted all day. Columbus's ship began to sink. He and the other sailors had to jump into the sea.

They were a long way from shore. Columbus began to swim. He saw an oar and grabbed it. He swam and floated for a long time. At last he landed on the shore.

Columbus had landed in the country of Portugal. Columbus knew God had brought him to Portugal.

Ships brought spices to Europe. The people in Europe liked the pepper, cinnamon, cloves and other spices. The spices made their food taste better. Spices also kept the food from spoiling.

The spices came from far away in Asia. They were from the countries of India, China, and Cipango. Those lands were called the Indies.

Traders came from Asia. They traveled across the mountains and deserts of Asia in a caravan. They brought the spices and other goods to the Mediterranean Sea. There they were loaded on the ships which sailed to the seaports in Europe.

Prince Henry, of Portugal, had decided that it would be better to sail around Africa to reach the Indies. That would be easier than the long, hard trip across the continent.

Sailors were not prepared for the long voyage around Africa. So Prince Henry began a school for sailors. The school taught about sailing, making maps and charts, and using a compass. The compass helped the sailors know where they were, even when it was dark. Prince Henry knew this would help the sailors not be afraid of such a long voyage. Soon the people of Portugal knew more about sailing than the people from any other country.

God had brought Columbus to Portugal for a special reason. Columbus decided to stay in Portugal where he could learn more about sailing. He lived near the city of Lisbon. Lisbon was a busy seaport.

Columbus married a lady in Lisbon and they had a son, named Diego.

Columbus's father-in-law had been a sailor. He had many charts and papers. Columbus studied the maps and charts. Columbus learned about new places and how to find them. He saw large parts of the ocean where no one had sailed. No one knew what was there.

Columbus knew the earth was round. He decided ships could reach India by sailing west. He thought this would be easier than going across mountains and deserts. He also thought it would be easier than Prince Henry's plan to sail the long distance around Africa.

Columbus began to draw maps showing Europe, Asia, and Africa. He did not know how big the earth really was. He did not know how large the Atlantic Ocean was.

He, also, did not know God had made two continents to the west of Europe. These continents blocked the path from Europe to Asia. No one in Europe knew about the continents of North America and South America.

Columbus believed God wanted him to sail west to the Indies. It was good that Columbus did not know how large the ocean was. It was good that he did not know how big the earth was. If he had known, he might not have made the voyage.

Finding a Way

Columbus decided to sail west, around the globe, to the Indies. But Columbus did not own a ship. He did not have money to hire a ship. He did not have money to hire sailors to sail the ship. He needed help to make his plan work.

Christopher Columbus

Columbus asked the King of Portugal to help him. Columbus told the King he would find a route to the East. He said it would take less time than sailing around Africa.

The King had no faith in Columbus's idea. He knew the voyage would cost a great sum. He did not want to help Columbus. But Columbus did not give up.

In 1485, Columbus's wife died. Columbus and his son left Portugal. They went to Spain.

King Ferdinand and Queen Isabella ruled Spain. They always wanted to do what was best for Spain.

When he arrived in Spain, Columbus met a duke. The duke liked Columbus's idea to sail west to find the Indies. He wanted to help Columbus. He said he would provide ships for the trip.

The duke told King Ferdinand and Queen Isabella about Columbus's plan. Queen Isabella liked the idea. She wanted to see Columbus. She asked him to meet her in Cordova.

Columbus packed his things and went to Cordova. But the King and Queen were very busy. They did not have time to think about new ideas, because Spain was fighting a war.

For two years Columbus stayed in Spain. He kept trying to meet the King and Queen. He met many men. Some thought his ideas were good. Others laughed at him.

Columbus met one of the church leaders. This man served the King and Queen. The church leader thought the King and Queen should listen to Columbus. He wanted to help Columbus.

At last the King and Queen sent for Columbus. They listened to his plan and liked it. But they were still busy with the war. They could not plan for anything else. They asked Columbus to wait.

Columbus waited in Spain. Time passed and Columbus wanted an answer. He asked some other men to talk with the King and Queen. The King and Queen sent word to Columbus that they must wait until the war was over. Then they would think about new things.

Christopher Columbus

After six years, Columbus thought the King and Queen wanted to be rid of him. He thought he had wasted all of his time in Spain. He and Diego packed their things. They planned to leave Spain.

Near Palos, Columbus and his son Diego stopped at a house to beg for some food and drink. Priests lived in the house. They talked with Columbus. Columbus told them of his plan for sailing to the Indies.

One of the priests had thought much about sailing. He liked to study maps and charts. He wanted to learn about the earth. He thought Columbus's idea was good.

The priest sent for other wise men from Palos to talk with Columbus. They listened to Columbus. They thought he had a good plan.

One man, Martin Alonzo Pinzon, said he would help Columbus. He was a rich man. He was willing to go with Columbus to see the King and Queen once more.

The priest knew the Queen well. He wrote to the Queen. He begged Columbus to stay in Palos until the Queen answered. Columbus liked Spain. He decided to wait.

After two weeks, the Queen sent an answer. She asked the priest to come at once to the court. She said that Columbus might hope to have an answer soon.

The priest hurried to the Queen. He pled for Columbus. He told the Queen that he was sure Columbus's plan would work.

The Queen listened to the priest. She asked for Columbus to come at once. She even sent money to pay for the cost of his trip. She also gave him money to buy some new clothes.

Finally, Columbus stood before King Ferdinand and

Queen Isabella. Once again he told the King and Queen his plans.

The Queen asked Columbus what he wanted for a reward. He told them he wanted part of any gold, silver, pearls, or spices which he found. He wanted to govern any new lands he would find. He also wanted to be called Admiral of the Ocean Sea.

Columbus said he would pay an eighth of the expenses. He asked that the King and Queen pay the rest.

The King and Queen and their wise men thought Columbus asked too much. But Columbus knew that what he had asked was just. Again the Queen said she needed to think about it.

Columbus left the royal court once more. He was very sad. He thought he must leave Spain.

Some friends, who believed in Columbus's plan, went to the King and Queen. The friends told them that it would be a great loss for Spain if they did not help Columbus.

The King could not see any good in the plan. He had to think about the many other costs from the war.

The Queen was moved at the words that were given. She knew that Columbus had a grand plan. She knew it would be good for Spain.

The Queen was quiet for a while. Then she looked up and said, "I will pledge my jewels to raise the funds."

Queen Isabella sent a man to bring Columbus back. When he learned what the Queen had promised, he hurried to her.

They agreed upon all of the terms. The King and Queen signed the paper on April 17, 1492.

Much work had to be done. Three ships had to be found. Seamen must be found who were willing to make the voyage.

The Great Adventure

Columbus began to seek ships and crews for the voyage. Bold men shrank from making the voyage Columbus had planned. They were afraid of the unknown ocean. After weeks, Columbus had not found even one ship.

Christopher Columbus

At last, Martin Alonzo Pinzon decided he and his brother would join Columbus. They would provide one of the ships.

Once the Pinzons planned to join Columbus, others were willing to make the voyage. Some were sent on the voyage by the King and Queen.

Finally, Columbus had three ships — Nina, Pinta, and the Santa Maria. The three ships were small to make such a long voyage. Columbus thought it would help to have small ships. They would be able to sail close to the shores. They would also be able to sail in shallow rivers.

On Friday, August 3, 1492, Columbus set sail. He steered the ships for the Canary Islands. He planned to sail west from the Canary Islands.

Some of the sailors were afraid. They did not want to make the voyage. Columbus thought they might insist on returning to Spain.

On the third day, the Pinta sent a signal to Columbus. There was a problem with the rudder. Columbus thought this was a trick to have the ship return to Spain. Martin Pinzon repaired the ship and they sailed on to the Canary Islands.

Columbus spent three weeks in the Canary Islands. He searched for a ship to replace the Pinta. He could not find a ship that could cross the ocean. Finally they made a new part for the Pinta.

On September 6, the three ships sailed from the Canary Islands. For three days, there was no wind. They could still see the Canary Islands.

On the third day, a breeze came. The sails were filled. They sailed west away from the land they knew.

Columbus was happy that they were on their way. But many of the sailors were afraid when they could not see the land. Some of the men cried. They had left their families and friends.

They did not know if they would ever see their homes again.

Columbus tried to soothe them. He told them of the countries they would see. He promised them land and riches.

Columbus kept a journal each day. He planned for the King and Queen to read the journal when he returned. He wrote about the birds they saw and the weather.

On September 14, some birds flew around the ship. They were birds that stayed close to land. They saw some weeds floating in the ocean. The men thought they must be near land. But Columbus did not think they were near the Indies.

There was no land and they kept on sailing west. The wind was blowing from the east to the west and moved their ships west. The men were afraid that there would be no wind going east when they were ready to return to Spain.

On September 20, the wind blew from the southwest. This cheered the men. They knew the wind did not always blow from the east.

Days went by and there still was no land. The men began to think they would never find land. They thought they would be lost in the ocean. They thought they would never be able to return to Spain.

On September 25, Martin Alonzo Pinzon cried, "Land! Land! Senor I claim my reward!" He pointed to the southwest, where it seemed there was land. Columbus and the crew rejoiced. Columbus fell on his knees to thank God. Pinzon and some of his men sang a hymn. But, the next morning, they saw there was no land. It must have been a cloud.

The King and Queen had promised a prize to the person who saw the land first. Each of the crew wanted to have the prize. Each time they thought they saw land, they would cry out.

Columbus finally told the men they must not cry "Land!" unless they were sure. If they cried "Land!"

and land was not found in three days, they would not share in the prize.

On October 6, they thought they saw land. But there was no land. On October 7, they thought they saw land. But there was no land.

Day after day, the men saw birds and plants in the water. They no longer had faith in these signs. They begged Columbus to turn back and give up.

Columbus told them they must go on. The King and Queen had sent them to find the Indies. He was sure that this could be done.

October 11 brought more signs of land. Weeds that grow in rivers were seen floating on the water. There was a branch with berries on it. They found a small board which had been carved. Each man began to watch closely. Each wanted to be the first to see the land.

As darkness came, Columbus was walking on the high deck of the ship. About ten o'clock, he thought he saw a light a long way off. Two other men saw the light.

The light seemed to move. They thought it might be a torch carried by someone in a boat. Or perhaps it was being carried from house to house.

The ships kept sailing. About two o'clock in the morning, the Pinta shot a gun. All of the men heard the cry, "Land! Land!"

"Land! Land!"

On Friday morning, October 12, Columbus first saw the New World. As dawn came, he saw an island covered with trees. The people of the island were running to the shore.

Christopher Columbus

The anchors were dropped. Columbus put on a rich, red suit. He took the flag of Spain. Columbus, Pinzon, and others rowed small boats to shore.

When Columbus reached the shore, he fell to his knees. He kissed the earth and thanked God.

Columbus claimed the land for King Ferdinand and Queen Isabella of Spain. He named the island San Salvador.

Columbus thought he had landed on one of the islands of India. He called the natives Indians.

The natives were friendly. They had no swords. They had no guns. They only had lances. The end of the lance was sharp.

Columbus was kind to the natives. Many of the Indians had small pieces of gold. They traded the gold for beads and bells.

Columbus asked the Indians where they found their gold. They pointed south.

Columbus thought he was on the islands near Cathay, in the China Sea.

For weeks, Columbus sailed from island to island. On December 24, the Santa Maria was wrecked on the coast of Haiti. Columbus called the island Hispaniola.

Columbus knew the ship could never sail again. He had a new plan. The ship's wood was used to build a fort.

Some of the men chose to stay at the fort and begin a new colony. The men were to look for mines. They were to learn the ways of the natives. They planned for other ships and men from Spain to join them.

Home to Spain

After months in the New World, Columbus began the long journey home. On January 4, 1493, Columbus sailed from Haiti on the Nina. They sailed into a bad storm. The winds blew. They thought that all would be lost.

Columbus wanted others to know of his discovery. He wrote about their voyage. He told of the new lands he had claimed for King Ferdinand and Queen Isabella. He made a second copy of his writing. He sealed both copies in wax and put each in a barrel. One of the barrels was thrown into the sea. He put the second barrel on the deck. If their ship sank, the barrel might float to shore.

On February 17, the ship reached an island owned by Portugal.

The King of Portugal was not happy that Columbus's voyage had been a success. The new lands could have been owned by Portugal. But he had not liked Columbus's plan. He ordered Columbus and his men to be taken as prisoners.

At last, the King chose to honor and protect Columbus. They sailed on toward Spain.

Columbus returned to the port of Palos. There was great joy when the people learned of the discovery of new lands.

A grand parade was formed. Columbus and his men went to the church to give thanks to God. Bells were rung and people shouted with joy when they saw Columbus.

In April, Columbus arrived in Barcelona. King Ferdinand and

Queen Isabella received him with great honor. As Columbus came toward them, the King and Queen rose. They asked Columbus to be seated while he told them of his discoveries. This was a rare honor.

Columbus told of the most important events. When he had finished, the King and Queen sank to their knees. They thanked God for His Providence. All who were there joined them. The court of Spain gave God the glory for the discovery of new lands.

Link to the New World

Columbus made four voyages to the new lands he had found. But, he never knew that these were the continents of North America and South America. He never knew that he had found the New World.

God had prepared Christopher Columbus to find a path across the unknown sea. God used Columbus to open the door to the New World.

Chapter 13
The Earliest Settlement in the New World

Jamestown

Christopher Columbus opened the way to the New World in 1492. But, the continent of North America was found in 1497 by John Cabot. He was an explorer from England.

The English claimed North America for their country. But there were no English colonies in the New World until nearly 100 years later.

Sir Walter Raleigh sailed to North America in 1578. He hoped to settle the first colony in the New World. He brought men with him. But the colony did not last.

Many English ships sailed to the New World to trade and fish.

In 1607, King James I wrote a charter for an English colony in North America. The king planned the civil government of the colony. He did not plan for self government. The people could not choose their own rulers. The king chose men to control the colony.

The king made a long list of rules for the colony. He ordered that the Church of England should be the only church. Any money the colonists earned from trade would be kept together. No person could earn money for himself.

Men settled in the King's colony, Virginia. They found a river which they

Jamestown

named the James River in honor of King James. They named their colony Jamestown.

The first men who came to Jamestown were not ready to live in the new country. Many of them were not used to hard work. They did not bring their families. They planned to find riches and adventure, and then return to England.

When the ships returned to England, the colonists were left with very few supplies. They had to eat poor food. The climate was different from that of England. Half of the men died before autumn.

The men begged John Smith, one of the colonists, to lead them. He told the men to build huts for the winter.

He gave the men different tasks. He told some to mow. Others bound the thatch. Others built the houses. Others thatched them. John Smith always worked harder than any of the other men.

John Smith also explored the land. He became a friend to some of the Indians. He bought supplies from the Indians.

Once when John Smith traveled up the river, he was captured by unfriendly Indians. These Indians had killed several men from Jamestown.

John Smith gave the Indian king a compass. He showed the Indians all the wonderful things the compass could do.

The Indians tied John Smith to a tree and planned to shoot him. When the king held up the compass in his hand, they did not shoot John Smith.

Jamestown

The Indians kept John Smith as their prisoner. They marched him from place to place.

At last they came to Powhatan's village. The Indians dragged John Smith to a large stone, where they planned to kill him. Powhatan's young daughter, Pocahontas, held John Smith's head in her lap. She begged the Indians not to kill him. Because the Indian princess was so brave and kind, John Smith was saved.

God softened the hearts of the Indians. At last they let John Smith go back to Jamestown. The Indians even promised to be friends with the men at Jamestown. Pocahontas often came to visit Jamestown. Sometimes she brought corn for the men.

John Smith worked hard to lead Jamestown. He dreamed of a great colony in the New

World. Other men came from England. The colony grew to five hundred people.

John Smith explored nearby places and made maps of Virginia. Then he was badly injured and had to return to England.

More colonists arrived in Jamestown. But the settlers did not govern themselves well. They did not work hard. They were wasteful. Soon all of their supplies were gone. In less than six months, there were only sixty people left in the colony.

The colonists did not know what to do. They decided to go back to England. But, God would not let the work in Virginia be lost. Just as their ships reached the mouth of the James River, three new ships from England met them. These ships brought fresh supplies, tools, provisions, and new settlers for the colony.

The Jamestown colony grew. The settlers learned that each family must plant their own crops. The people worked harder when they could keep their own produce.

The Jamestown colonists found a way to live in the New World. John Smith's dream had come true.

John Smith's Map of Virginia

The Indian girl Pocahontas grew to be a woman. John Rolfe, one of the English settlers, loved her, and they were married. Pocahontas was baptized in the little church at Jamestown.

More people in England heard about Jamestown. Some decided to settle in the New World. John Smith's maps helped them find a place to live. His hard work prepared the way for others to come to America.

Chapter 14
The Pilgrims

Seed of our Christian Republic

During the two hundred years after John Wycliffe's Bible, the English people had been studying God's Word.

God's Word taught the people that they were sinners. They also learned that each person must come to God by faith in Jesus Christ. Through the reading of the Bible, God changed their hearts and showed them how to live.

The King was in control of the Church of England. He decided what was right for the churches to teach. Godly people soon found that some of the things being taught in the King's church were not right.

The Separatists

They read in the New Testament that the early Christians started churches in many places. They decided they should be able to have their own churches. They did not want to be part of the Church of England, the King's church, any more. They were called Separatists, because they separated from the Church of England.

A small group of Separatists in Scrooby left the Church of England. They formed their own church. Their pastor was Pastor John Robinson.

The King did not want any churches in the land except the Church of England. He made it very hard

for the Separatists to have their own churches. At last, the King said they must return to the Church of England or leave the country.

By 1607, the year that Jamestown was started, the people in the church at Scrooby decided they should leave England. They made plans to go to Holland.

The Separatists knew life in Holland would be difficult. The people in Holland did not speak English. They spoke the Dutch language. Many Separatist men were farmers in England. They knew they could not be farmers in Holland. Life in Holland would be very hard. But, the Separatists believed God would take care of them.

The King was angry that the Separatists did not do what he wanted. The King tried to keep them from leaving England. But God helped the Separatists, and, at last, they arrived safely in Holland.

Holland

Life was quite hard for the Separatists in Holland. But they were glad to be free to worship God in their own church, as the Bible taught them to do.

The Separatists worked hard at their jobs in Holland, but they were very poor. Because the Separatists were so honest, the Dutch people soon learned to trust them. The Dutch liked to hire them for jobs. They knew the Separatists would work their best.

The small group of Separatists stayed in Holland for about twelve years. During that time, they heard about the Jamestown colony in America.

Since life was so difficult in Holland, the Separatists agreed it would be better for them to go to the New World. They also wanted to tell the people of America about the Gospel of Jesus Christ.

Some of the men from the church began to make plans for the trip to America. Each family had to decide whether or not they should go to the New World. Some decided to stay in Holland.

Since the Separatists were going to such a faraway place, they were called Pilgrims. They were sad to leave, but hoped for a better life in America.

Pastor John Robinson chose to stay in Holland with the families who did not leave. He planned to come to America at a later time.

Perhaps the Separatists wondered what it would be like to cross the ocean and live in the New World. They knew that God would take care of them and help them.

The Separatists needed more people to go with them to America. Some who joined them were not Christians.

The journey to America cost a great deal. A company of men, called the London Company, loaned part of the money to the Pilgrims. The Pilgrims promised to repay the money by sending furs and wood back to England.

The London Company said that the Pilgrims must own everything as a group. When they planted crops, hunted, or cut wood to send to England, it would all belong to the whole group. The families would have to share everything.

To America

Two ships were hired to take the Pilgrims to America. The two ships were the Mayflower and the Speedwell. The Pilgrims knew it would take eight or nine weeks to sail to America. At last, everything was ready for the voyage.

The ships had not sailed far when the Speedwell began to leak. The Captain sailed to a nearby port to repair the ship. But the crew decided the Speedwell could not make the long voyage.

When some of the people heard that the Speedwell could not continue, they decided to stay in England. Others moved onto the Mayflower. On September 6, 1620, the Mayflower finally left England for America.

The voyage across the ocean was very hard. There were so many storms that the captain would not let

The Pilgrims

the Pilgrims walk on the deck of the ship. They had to stay in the lower deck. It was very crowded and they did not have fresh air.

When the storms were bad, the crew and the Pilgrims did not know whether their ship would even make it to America. The Pilgrims could only pray for God to protect them.

God answered their prayers, and, at last, they arrived in America.

The King of England had told the Pilgrims they could settle in the north part of Virginia. When the Mayflower came to land, it was not in Virginia. The Pilgrims learned that they were at Cape Cod. At first, they thought they could sail south to Virginia. Their plans did not work. God wanted them to stay in Cape Cod.

It was November 11, 1620, when the Pilgrims arrived at Cape Cod. There were no friends to welcome them to the new land. There were no houses where they could stay. They knew that winter would be coming soon. The men began to look for a place to build their houses.

They found a place where an Indian village had been. No Indians were living there. The trees had been cleared, so the Pilgrims were able to begin building. They knew that God had led them to this place. Later, the Pilgrims named the colony Plymouth.

The Pilgrims

Since the Pilgrims were not in Virginia, they were not under the control of the King. The rules he had given them were only for Virginia. Some of the men, who were not Christians, thought there would be no laws.

The Pilgrims knew that the colony must have civil government. They had learned how to govern their church in England and in Holland. They also knew that they could plan the government for their new colony.

The men wrote a set of rules for Plymouth. It was called the Mayflower Compact. All of the men signed the compact and agreed to live by the rules. The Mayflower Compact gave the colony a plan for their civil government. They chose a governor for the colony.

The Pilgrims began to build a storehouse. Then they began to build some small cottages. The winter weather made their work hard.

The winter was a very difficult time. Because of the cold weather, the poor food, and the hard work, many of the Pilgrims became sick.

At first, those who were well kept working and took care of those that were sick. More and more people became sick.

At one time, only six or seven people were well enough to take care of all those who were sick. They cooked for the ones who were sick, washed their clothes, and made their beds. They did each of these tasks willingly and cheerfully.

Sometimes two or three people died in one day. So many people died that they were buried together on a hill near the harbor. By the end of February, only 50 people were left out of the 100 who had settled in Plymouth.

When the weather became a little warmer, the sick began to get well. Then they were able to work again.

Sometimes the Pilgrims saw Indians hiding in the trees. The Indians watched them building their houses. Once, when they left to go eat dinner, the Indians stole their tools.

About March 16, an Indian walked into their village and spoke to them in English. They were very surprised that he knew their language. The Indian's name was Samoset.

Samoset wanted the Pilgrims and Indians to be friends. The Pilgrims were kind to Samoset. He brought back the tools that the Indians had stolen.

Samoset told them about Squanto. Squanto was from the Indian tribe that had lived right where the Pilgrims were building their houses. Squanto had been taken to England and, while he was gone, all of his tribe had died from a sickness. Samoset told the Pilgrims that he would ask Squanto to come help them.

Squanto could speak English much better than Samoset could. Squanto became a special friend to the

Pilgrims. Samoset and Squanto brought the Indian chief to meet the Pilgrims. His name was Massasoit. The Pilgrims and Massasoit made promises to each other. They promised they would not harm each other or steal one another's things. These promises made peace between the Pilgrims and the Indians. They kept the promises for at least fifty years.

When spring came, the Mayflower was ready to sail back to England. The captain knew how hard the winter had been. He told the Pilgrims they could sail back with him. But, not one of the Pilgrims would leave. They knew God had led them to stay in Plymouth.

With Squanto's help, the Plymouth colonists worked hard to plant many crops. The seeds from England did not grow well in this new land. Squanto taught them how to plant corn. He also taught them how to take care of the corn so it would grow well. When fall came, they had a very small harvest.

In time, more people came to live in the Plymouth colony. The new colonists did not bring proper supplies with them. Although the Pilgrim colonists barely had enough for their own families, they shared their food, clothes, tools and homes with the new colonists.

Building a colony in the New World was very difficult. The colonists did not have enough food. At one time, each person had only a little bit of bread to eat every day. They thought they might starve.

After two years, the people of Plymouth knew that they could not live without more food. They began to think about how they could raise more corn. The governor and other wise men decided upon a new

plan. Each family should have its own field. The food that they grew would belong to their own family. The food did not have to be divided for the whole colony.

This new plan worked much better than the old one. Now the people were more willing to work in the fields. Each one knew that if he worked hard, he would have more food for his family.

Soon the people were looking forward to the best crop Plymouth had ever had.

In spite of their hard work, the crops began to suffer. From the third week of May until July, there was

no rain. It was very hot. The crops were too dry. The Pilgrims knew that if rain did not come, the crops would die. If the crops died, the colonists would starve during the winter.

Prayer for Rain

The Pilgrims set aside a special day to pray for rain. God gave them an answer. In the morning and most of the day it was clear and very hot. There was not even a cloud in the sky. But, late in the day, it began to rain. There was no wind nor thunder. The rain came down gently, watering the dry, thirsty plants.

The colonists knew God had sent the rain. The Indians were amazed. They saw that God was powerful and that He took care of His people.

With the rain and warm weather, the crops were able to grow. For the first time, the colonists had a great harvest.

The Pilgrims were thankful for God's answer to their prayers. They had a special day to thank God for His many blessings. They invited the Indians to come

to Plymouth for a day of thanksgiving. There were games to enjoy and plenty of food for everyone.

After this great harvest, the colony never had another famine. In time, more and more colonists came to Plymouth.

God used the Plymouth colony to teach others some important lessons. The most important lesson was that the new colonies in America could govern themselves. The king did not have to make rules for the colonies when the people governed themselves, their families, their churches, and their colony.

The self government in Plymouth was the beginning of a new nation, the United States of America.

Chapter 15
One Nation Under God

Soon after Plymouth was settled, many other colonies began along the east coast of North America.

More colonists came from England. Others came from Holland and Germany. They came from many kinds of churches.

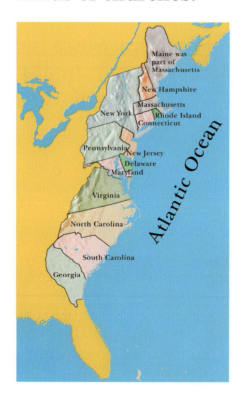

After 150 years, there were thirteen colonies in America. The thirteen colonies belonged to the country of England.

Since England was far away, each colony had its own civil government. The colonists had learned how to govern themselves. They knew that they could make and obey their own laws. They could choose the people to make the laws.

The thirteen colonies decided to form their own nation. Each colony chose representatives to meet in Philadelphia.

On July 4, 1776, the representatives approved the Declaration of Independence. The Declaration of Independence said that the colonies were now free states and no longer belonged to England.

The Declaration of Independence made the colonies a new nation, the United States of America. Since the Declaration of Independence was signed on July 4, 1776, we say that July 4 is our nation's birthday. We call this holiday Independence Day.

Chapter 16
George Washington

Father of Our Country

The colonists signed the Declaration of Independence in 1776. But England did not want the colonies to be independent. The King sent the English army to America. The colonies had to defend their independence.

God had prepared leaders in the colonies to help the Americans protect their liberty. One of these leaders was George Washington.

George Washington was born in the Virginia colony in 1732, forty-four years before the Declaration of Independence. His family lived in the country. While he was a boy, he learned about plants and animals. He also was taught good manners. His parents taught him to love God and obey the Bible.

George Washington learned to write down the things he studied. He was careful in his writing and liked to learn new things. He wrote in special notebooks. Today, some of his notebooks are in the Library of Congress.

George Washington's father was a surveyor. He measured land. Then he made drawings showing each person's land.

When George was only eleven years old, his father died. Later, George Washington found his father's surveying tools and learned surveying. By the time he was sixteen, George Washington was such a good surveyor that he was hired to help survey the wilderness. He traveled far away from home. Sometimes he even saw Indians. He learned about the land and rivers of the American wilderness. This was a special time for the young man.

When George Washington was twenty-one, the colonies still belonged to England. Washington joined the English army. The Governor of Virginia asked Washington to take a message to a French settlement in the Ohio Valley, near Lake Erie. Washington chose men to make the trip with him. The trip lasted over two months and took them over mountains and through Indian territory. Along the way, they met many Indians. Some of the Indians they met were friendly and some were not.

George Washington wrote about the trip in a journal. He told about the cold weather, ice and snow. There were no houses, so they had to camp outside. Once, when they were crossing a river, they fell from their raft into the icy cold water. That night they had to sleep outside without even a fire.

At last, the long trip was over. Washington returned to Virginia with an answer for the Governor. The French were trying to take the land that England had claimed. This led to a war with the French. Because the Indians helped the French army, it was called the French and Indian War.

George Washington was an officer in the English army during the French and Indian War. Many of the men in the army had come from England and did not know how to fight the Indians. The English soldiers marched in rows through the forest and up the hills. The bright red coats of the English soldiers made easy targets for the Indians who hid behind the trees.

George Washington tried to explain a better way for the soldiers to fight, but the English general would not listen. In one battle, the English general and many of the soldiers were killed.

During that battle, George Washington was protected in a special way. Four bullets were shot through his coat, but he was not hurt. One Indian chief said, "He will never die in battle. I told all my braves to aim at him, but they could not hit him." God kept him safe because he had other work for Washington to do.

When the war was over, Washington returned to Virginia and his home at Mount Vernon. He loved farming and living at Mount Vernon. He planned to stay there. But this pleasant life at Mount Vernon did not last.

England taxed the Americans to force them to help pay for the French and Indian War. Because the Americans had no one to represent them in England, they were not willing to pay the taxes.

England sent soldiers to America to make the Americans pay the taxes. But the Americans knew they were right. They still would not pay the taxes.

In 1776, the Americans declared their independence. They had to be ready to fight the English army and defend the liberty to govern themselves. They asked George Washington to lead the American army.

George Washington trained the American army to fight in the war. The Americans did not have special uniforms. The only guns they had were the ones they used to hunt for meat.

The English army had nice, red uniforms. The English soldiers were called the redcoats. They had many guns and everything they needed to fight a war.

For six years the Americans fought the English.

Washington and his soldiers spent one winter at Valley Forge in Pennsylvania. It was a cold, snowy winter. The men did not have enough food. Their clothes were ragged. Their shoes were worn out. Many were sick.

Washington did not know how to help the suffering soldiers. He knew that God was in control of everything. One day, as a man walked through the woods, he saw someone kneeling in the snow. Walking closer, he could tell that the man was Washington. He heard

Washington pray for God to take care of the army and to help them fight for liberty.

The English and American soldiers fought many battles during the war. The last battle was at Yorktown, Virginia, in 1781. The English General Cornwallis made plans that he thought would help him win the battle. But God sent a storm that kept General Cornwallis's plans from working. When General Cornwallis knew he could not win, he signed a peace treaty. The war was over.

The redcoats marched out to meet George Washington and laid down their guns. The Americans were happy. The nation was free at last. They had fought long and hard for the liberty to govern themselves.

When the war was over, Washington went back to Mount Vernon. He thought he would stay at Mount Vernon for the rest of his life.

The American people were very happy to be at peace. They worked hard in their homes and shops.

As time went by, they realized that it would be best to make a plan for all the states to work together as one nation.

In 1787, representatives from the thirteen states went to a meeting in Philadelphia. George Washington was a representative from Virginia.

These representatives wrote the laws for the United States of America. The laws were called the Constitution. The representatives signed the Constitution and each of the thirteen states agreed to be governed by it.

The United States was the first nation in which the people governed themselves. They chose representatives to make the laws.

The Constitution said that the United States should have a President. The representatives of the people chose George Washington to be their President.

In 1789, George Washington became the first President of the United States of America. The people loved George Washington and were happy to have him as their President.

George Washington wanted to protect liberty for the people. He wanted the ideas of liberty and self government to always be a part of the new nation.

For eight years, George Washington served his country as President. Though the people wanted him to be President for four more years, he wanted to go back to Mount Vernon.

Washington loved being home again at Mount Vernon. He worked outdoors and watched the river, the trees, and the beautiful sunrises and sunsets.

In December, 1799, he was out in a storm for several hours. After coming home, he became very sick. The doctors tried to help Washington, but he only got

weaker. On December 14, 1799, Washington died at Mount Vernon, the home he loved.

When George Washington died, the whole country was saddened. They remembered the many important things Washington had done. He had helped the new nation become a land of liberty. He had led the American army. He had served as the first President of the United States of America.

Because of all he did for America, George Washington is called the *Father of our Country.*

One man said what the people of America felt about George Washington: "First in war, first in peace, and first in the hearts of his countrymen."

Chapter 17
Daniel Boone

God's Man for Opening the Western Frontier

In America's colonial days, George Washington and other Americans lived on farms and in the Eastern towns. They enjoyed the good houses which had been built and the land which had been cleared by their hard-working parents, grandparents and great-

grandparents. America was a place in which children could grow up, go to school, and one day become merchants, farmers, lawyers, musicians, and teachers.

Sometimes, in the evenings, the colonists sat down to rest from their long day's work. They talked about the lands in the west.

The Western lands were a new frontier. There were no houses, no towns, no farms with the trees cleared away for planting crops. There were only trees, wild animals, traveling Indian tribes, and a few forts.

The frontier was an interesting place. A few men thought they might like to go out west and build a new place for themselves and their families. But the job would require someone brave and skillful. A man on the frontier must be a friend to the Indians. He must protect himself from wild animals. He must find his own food and take care of himself in the wilderness.

Travelers had to cross mountains and face many dangers in order to see the western frontier. The colonists needed a pathway to the frontier. A path would make it easier for men and families to go west and build towns and farms. God had just the right person to find a path to the west. His name was Daniel Boone.

While Daniel Boone was a boy, God taught him the things he would need to know in order to be one of the first pioneers to go to the American frontier.

Daniel Boone was born in Pennsylvania in 1735. As a boy, Daniel's favorite place was the outdoors. He learned about animals by watching and listening. He imitated their sounds, and learned their habits. He liked to go hunting and fishing, and spent hours in the woods. He learned to be brave and strong.

When Daniel was eighteen, his family moved to North Carolina. God was preparing Daniel to be a pioneer leader. Daniel spent most of his time hunting. He collected furs and sold them in the Eastern settlements.

During the French and Indian war, Daniel joined the militia. At night, around the campfires, the men talked about interesting places. A man named John Finley told about his adventures in lands to the west. He liked the frontier lands and planned to return when he could. Daniel Boone was interested, too. He wanted a chance to travel in the frontier, where the woods were full of wild animals.

After serving in the militia, Daniel returned to North Carolina. He married Rebecca Bryan. She liked the frontier lands and would be a strong pioneer herself. They lived in a log cabin, on a farm in North Carolina. Daniel worked hard and often thought about what it would be like to travel west.

At last, in 1769, Daniel had his chance to explore the wilderness of Kentucky. John Finley, John Stewart, and three others travelled with Boone. They carried their rifles and axes with them. They set up a camp on the eastern side of the Cumberland Mountains.

The men explored for a few days. At last, they saw Kentucky. They thought the land was beautiful. They

were pleased to see elk, deer, and other wild animals. They saw a buffalo herd for the first time.

The men thought that things seemed large in the west. They saw all the land where families could travel and build new homes. Daniel Boone said, "Here both man and beast may grow to their full size."

Daniel Boone and his friends explored Kentucky for six months. Then Indians captured Daniel Boone and John Stewart.

The two captives marched with the Indians for seven days. Finally, they escaped and returned to their campsite. They were sad to find that their friends had given up and returned to their homes.

Daniel Boone did not give up. He and John Stewart continued to explore. They were surprised one day to find Squire Boone, Daniel's brother, and another man, searching for them in the wilderness.

Imagine how difficult it must have been for Squire Boone to find Daniel and John Stewart. Without any roads or signs to show the way, Squire Boone and his friend searched until they found the explorers.

Squire Boone wanted to explore the frontier with Daniel. He brought supplies from the settlement. Daniel was glad to have his brother's help. He was also grateful for the fresh gunpowder and lead. He knew that a pioneer must always watch for danger and hunt his own food.

These were men of courage, who would not give up. They found their own way. They followed paths made by animals, and left their own marks in the forest.

It wasn't long before Daniel and Squire Boone were alone in the Kentucky wilderness. They kept exploring until it was time to get more supplies. Then Daniel sent Squire back to the settlements and faced the wilderness alone.

Daniel was not afraid of Indians or wild animals. He watched constantly for any signs of danger.

Daniel Boone was not truly alone in the forest. He was surrounded by the trees and wild animals. Indians traveled in the forests as well. They sometimes tried to capture Daniel.

One day, Daniel watched as Indians came through the woods following his tracks. He did his best to get

away, but the Indians still came after him. Boone thought about how he might escape. He noticed a long, wild grapevine hanging from a tree. Daniel grasped the vine and swung himself far to one side. He quickly moved on, so the Indians could not find his trail.

The Indians followed his tracks until the tracks suddenly disappeared. Without any clues, they could not capture the mighty American warrior.

When Squire Boone returned to the forest, the two brothers began to make plans for a settlement. They chose a place with rich soil and woods full of wild animals. Then they returned to their homes and families in North Carolina.

Daniel had faced the wilderness with courage. Now he had to wait patiently. He must sell his farm and prepare for the move to Kentucky.

In 1773, five families, along with forty men, set out for Kentucky. All the supplies for their new homes were carried in wagons. A herd of cattle was driven along with them.

The pioneers were attacked by Indians. The Indians killed six men, including Daniel's son. The cattle were scattered and killed.

Shocked by the disaster, most of the travelers were afraid to go on. Only Daniel Boone and his family were steadfast to their dream of building a home in Kentucky.

In 1774, the governor of Virginia wanted to purchase land from the Indians. He needed someone to be his agent. It must be someone who knew the Indians, and someone the Indians could trust. Of course, the best man for the job was Daniel Boone. He met with the Indians and purchased land along the Kentucky River from them.

A pathway was needed for settlers to travel to this new land in Kentucky. Who could make a pathway in the wilderness? No one could do that better than Daniel Boone.

So Daniel Boone took on another important task. He cleared a pathway for settlers to travel across the mountains to Kentucky. This path is called the wilderness trail.

At last, in 1775, Daniel Boone was able to carry out the plan for which he had been working and waiting such a long time. He began a settlement, called Boonesborough, not far from the Kentucky River. The settlement included a fort and a tall wooden fence called a palisade. These helped protect the families who came to live there. Daniel Boone was finally at home in Kentucky.

Daniel still hunted and watched for Indians. He thought Kentucky was the best land in America. He worked hard so that others would settle in the west.

Daniel Boone loved American liberty. He encouraged the Kentucky settlers to govern themselves and choose good representatives.

The pioneer families that settled in Boonesborough were hard workers, independent, and brave. They cut down trees from the forest to build their log cabins. They cleared the land and grew crops on their farms. They showed great courage in times of danger.

The pioneers fought for their liberty when they were attacked by the Indians. Some died to keep Boonesborough safe. Following Daniel Boone's example, they did not give up.

After many years, Kentucky was no longer a wilderness. Farms and towns were built by the pioneers. In 1792, Kentucky became a state.

Daniel Boone believed that God had chosen him to settle the wilderness. He had done exactly that. He had shown others the way. At the end of his life he said, "God gave me a work to perform, and I have done my best."

Chapter 18
Keeping One Nation under God

Many people began to move west. Families traveled along the wilderness trail opened by Daniel Boone. Other trails were opened for families to move west. Some families went to Indiana. Some moved to the new lands of the Wisconsin Territory. Some went to Texas. Some even went further west.

The Pioneers packed everything they had into a covered wagon. Then they traveled for many weeks. Sometimes they walked for many miles. They traveled through good weather and bad weather. They were seeking a new home for their family.

New families arrived in America from other countries. They had a dream of a new home. Their dream included owning land. Many had never owned land.

Each family wanted to enjoy the liberty in America.

The United States of America was a new nation. It had been built upon the idea of self government.

As children were born, and new families came to America, each family needed to learn to govern themselves. They must care for their own families. They had responsibility for the new towns.

More and more people came to live in the new land. It was important that the ideas which formed the nation would be taught to the children and to the new families.

The nation grew. The time came when the people from the states in the north did not agree with the people from the south. The times were difficult. But the problems had to be settled.

God worked in the hearts of men to keep one nation under God.

Chapter 19
Abraham Lincoln

God prepared a special man for America during a very difficult time in her history. That man was President Abraham Lincoln. Abraham Lincoln's history was simple.

In about 1781 or 1782, the Lincoln family began their trek along the wilderness trail. Abraham Lincoln was a friend of Daniel Boone's. He followed Boone, moving his wife and children from Virginia to Kentucky. This Abraham Lincoln was the grandfather of President Abraham Lincoln.

Tom Lincoln, Abraham's son, moved to Hardin County, Kentucky. There he met Nancy Hanks. Nancy and her family had also traveled the wilderness trail from Virginia.

Tom and Nancy were married. They lived in a small log cabin. The floors were dirt. There was only one small window.

Chapter 19

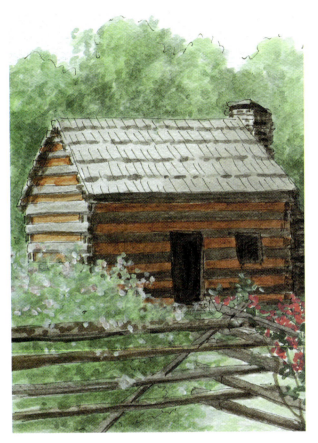

On February 12, 1809, a boy was born. No one knew that little Abraham would become the President of the United States. Little Abe had one older sister, Sarah.

Nancy Lincoln was a kind, gentle mother. She loved God and wanted her children to love Him. She taught them the Bible.

Abe learned to work hard. He had many chores. He carried water. He filled the woodbox with wood. He ran errands. He helped hoe weeds on the little farm. He and Sarah picked berries and hunted for nuts.

There was not much time for school. But Little Abe learned to read and write.

To Indiana

When Abe was about seven or eight years old, his family moved to Spencer County, Indiana. It was about the time Indiana became a state. It took many days to travel from Kentucky to Indiana.

When they arrived at their claim on Little Pigeon Creek, there was no house. The land had to be cleared of trees before a house could be built. The whole family helped to build the first cabin. It only had three sides. In the open side, they kept a fire burning day and night.

After a year, they built a new cabin. Tom chopped the logs. Nancy, Sarah, and Abe helped to trim the logs and clear the ground.

When they could go, Sarah and Abe had to walk nine miles to school. The many jobs on the farm kept them home much of the time.

When a sickness came to Little Pigeon Creek, mother Nancy died. It was a sad time for father Tom, Sarah, and Abe. They missed their mother very much. Little Sarah tried to cook and care for the family, but she was just a young girl.

After some time, Tom Lincoln headed back to Kentucky. There he planned to bring home a new mother for the children. Father was gone for several weeks. Abe and Sarah stayed in the cabin on Little Pigeon Creek.

One morning, there was a nice surprise. Father returned with his new wife, a mother for the children. He also brought Mrs. Lincoln's three children. They arrived with horses and a wagon. The wagon was filled with furniture and wonderful things for the cabin.

Instead of beds made from corn husks, they now had nice feather pillows and a feather mattress. There was also fine furniture.

The new mother loved Abe and his sister. She brought love and a mother's care back to the home.

Abe had learned to work hard. His father taught him how to care for the farm. But, more than anything, Abraham Lincoln loved to read. The Bible, Aesop's Fables, Pilgrim's Progress, and a life of Washington, he read over and over. There were not many books, but he read every book he could find. He always enjoyed the proverbs found in the Bible, and the fables written by Aesop. Later, Lincoln would become known for telling many fables to teach an idea to others.

Once Lincoln borrowed a book from a neighbor. When he was ready to go to sleep, he put the book in a crack between the logs. Rain came that night and soaked the book. Lincoln went to the neighbor and worked several days to pay for the book.

Lincoln loved to listen to the men as they talked about the nation. He enjoyed learning about Washington and Jefferson. He loved to hear stories. And he loved new words.

Abe grew quite tall. He was nearly six feet, four inches. It seemed that he was taller than all of the other boys and men in the settlement. His stepmother teased him about how tall he was. She told him to keep his hair clean, or he would get dirt on the ceiling.

One day, Abe decided to tease his stepmother. He had some children put their feet in the mud. Then he held them upside down. They walked on the ceiling, leaving their footprints.

Mrs. Lincoln laughed at the joke. Abe laughed. But then he cleaned the ceiling.

As he grew, he was very strong. Though he did not enjoy the farm work, he worked hard. When Abe's father did not need him, he worked for other families. Folks said that he could split logs better than any other.

To Illinois

When Abraham was twenty-one, his father decided to move to Illinois. Several families traveled in February of 1830. With wagons loaded, men walking alongside their wagons, they again moved west. At the Indiana-Illinois border, they crossed the Wabash River. The water was very cold.

There is a story told about Lincoln. When they reached the Illinois side of the river, Lincoln looked back to the Indiana side. There on the river bank was a dog. He was whining and running back and forth, but would not jump into the river and swim across. Lincoln waded across the icy water, and carried the dog over.

Lincoln helped his father build a log cabin and a fence. He then set out on his own. He wrapped all of his things in a bag, and left to make his own living.

To earn money for brown jeans, Lincoln split four hundred rails for each yard of cloth. Perhaps he wished he was not so tall and needed so much cloth.

Lincoln soon became a clerk in a country store. There were not many customers. Abe could spend much time reading. He was learning the many things he had not learned in school.

Abe Lincoln was always known for his honesty. Once, he gave a customer in the store the wrong change. He walked several miles that night to return the money. Soon people were calling him "Honest Abe."

Lincoln became the postmaster in New Salem. The post office was in a grocery store. People picked up their mail from Lincoln. Often when Abe had a letter for someone, he would put the letter in his hat. When he saw the person, he would give them their mail.

For the rest of his life, Lincoln carried many things in his hat. He would carry his handkerchief, letters, important papers, or notes for a speech he was writing.

Lincoln, like Washington, learned to be a surveyor. He taught himself surveying. People liked Lincoln. They enjoyed his speeches, stories, and witty sayings. They liked his honesty and good nature.

Public Life

Everybody around New Salem knew Abe Lincoln. They liked the young man in his tall hat. He always stopped to talk with them. In 1834, they elected Lincoln to the Illinois legislature. He was only twenty five years old. He walked one hundred miles to Springfield.

While in Springfield, Lincoln began to study law. Lincoln read many books to learn the law. He did not have to attend a special school.

In 1837, Lincoln began his life as a lawyer. He traveled the *circuit*. This meant he had to travel from one court to another in his horse and buggy.

Lincoln quickly became successful as a lawyer. He did not want to represent any case where the claim was not just. If he was convinced his client was right, he would usually win his case.

Lincoln always presented his case clearly. He could always keep the attention of the court and jury. He never charged more than he thought his service was worth. He would not take money from someone who was poor.

People enjoyed going to court to hear Lincoln. He could always make them understand. He also made them laugh.

President Abraham Lincoln

In 1860, Abraham Lincoln was elected as President of the United States. He was sad to leave Springfield. He knew he must depend upon God to lead him and the United States. There were great problems facing the nation.

In the South, there were many families who owned slaves. The slaves were used to care for the great plantations. When the Constitution was written, it was decided that each state should decide how to free their slaves. As time passed, the states did not do anything about the slaves.

As the nation grew, there was a question about the new states. Would they be allowed to have slaves?

Lincoln did not want slavery in the new states. He knew that "all men were created equal."

But most of all, Lincoln thought the nation should be saved. When Lincoln became President, he said that they must rely on God to care for them. In one famous speech, he quoted from the Bible, "A house divided against itself cannot stand."

After Lincoln was elected President, many Southern States decided they did not want to be part of the United States. They formed a new government, which they called *The Confederate States of America.*

The Northern States said they could not be a separate nation.

In April, 1861, guns were fired. A war began between the North and the South. Both sides were brave. Great battles were fought. Families were divided. Some fought for the North. Some fought for the South.

It was a sad, dark day in America. Lincoln felt his job was to save the United States. Finally, he decided he must free the slaves. He declared the slaves free. At last, all men were to be free.

This did not end the war. Many battles were fought. Many soldiers died.

Lincoln was asked to make a speech to honor the men who fought in the great battle at Gettysburg. He ended his speech with these words: "that this nation, under God, shall have a new birth of freedom—and that this government of the people, by the people, for the people, shall not perish from the earth."

After four years, the terrible war finally ended. The United States was to stay as one nation. The soldiers headed home.

God had used Lincoln to lead the American people through these difficult times.

But Lincoln would not live to enjoy the times of peace. A man shot him as he watched a play in Ford Theater, April 14, 1865. He died the next day.

People from the North and South had learned to love Lincoln. It was a sad time for the nation.

Chapter 20
Communication across a Nation

Since the beginning of our nation, the people knew that they must agree about the way the nation was to be governed. In order to agree, the people had to communicate with each other.

Many letters were written from colony to colony, and then from state to state. The letters shared people's ideas about the new government. Mothers and fathers, and even boys and girls, wrote letters. Books and tracts were written about civil government. Newspapers also included articles about civil government.

The people of America had joined together in a new nation. This new nation did not have a king. The people of America had learned that they could

govern themselves and choose the people for the job of civil government.

Noah Webster grew up during the time the nation was being formed. He was a young boy when the Declaration of Independence was written. As a young man, he read articles, books and tracts about civil government.

Noah Webster saw that words needed to be spelled the same each time. That way everyone would understand exactly what each word was. He wrote his *Blue-backed Speller* to help all Americans spell words correctly.

Noah Webster also knew that many words which had been used in England meant something different in America. In 1828, he wrote the first dictionary of the American language. This dictionary helped everyone understand what each word meant.

Mr. Webster knew that as the people wrote letters and books about civil government that they must each know the meaning of words. If people all used words in the same way, they would be able to understand one another's ideas better.

As the nation grew and many people moved further west, it took longer and longer for letters, books, or newspapers to reach them. Sometimes the people wished news could travel faster.

Samuel F. B. Morse

God used Samuel F. B. Morse to invent a way to send news anywhere in less than a minute.

Samuel Morse was born in Charlestown, Massachusetts, in 1791, about a mile from the place where Benjamin Franklin had been born. His full name was Samuel Finley Breese Morse. As a boy, he was always called Finley. As he grew older, he used the name Samuel F. B. Morse.

Samuel's father, Dr. Jedediah Morse, was the pastor of the First Congregational Church in Charlestown, Massachusetts. Dr. Morse loved learning. At age 23, he wrote the first geography published in America. When he was older, he wrote two books of American history.

Dr. Morse wanted his son Samuel to be a good student. Samuel found it very difficult to pay attention to his lessons. He liked drawing pictures and investigating new things much better.

When he was fourteen, Samuel passed the test to become a student at Yale College. Of all his studies at Yale, he liked science class the best. Benjamin Franklin had discovered electricity. Scientists were working to find some use for it. This interested Samuel.

While in college, Samuel continued to draw and paint. When he graduated from Yale, he asked his parents if he could study art in Europe. Samuel's parents did not want him to be an artist. They did not think he could earn a living as an artist.

Some American artists were invited to look at examples of Samuel's art. They thought his pictures were good. This helped his parents decide that Samuel should travel to Europe.

Samuel traveled to England to study painting with Benjamin West. Benjamin West, an American artist, had become President of the Royal Academy of London. Benjamin West trained many of the early American artists.

Samuel F. B. Morse became a good artist. He returned to America, where he continued to paint. Most of his pictures were portraits.

While Samuel painted for a living, he still wanted to learn everything he could about electricity and how people were trying to use it. He thought that electricity could be used to send messages. That way it would not take weeks for news to travel from one place to another.

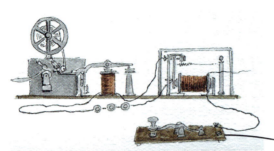

In 1829, Samuel Morse again traveled to Europe to study more about painting. He returned in 1832 on the ship Sully. On the long voyage, Samuel talked with other men about experiments with electricity which were being done in France. He kept talking about electricity. He thought a machine might be invented which could send written messages from one place to another.

Samuel thought about this so much he could not sleep at night. At last, he knew how he could make such a machine.

It took many years to make the invention work. During that time, Samuel Morse painted pictures to earn money to buy food. Sometimes he had to go hungry.

Samuel Morse's machine was connected to a wire a mile long. A pencil was fastened to the further end. He used his new machine to send electricity through the wire. The electricity made the pencil draw marks on a paper. He had invented the *electric telegraph*. He knew that if he could do this over a mile of wire, he could do it over a hundred or even a thousand miles of wire. At last, he had found the way for messages to be sent immediately from one place to another.

Before the telegraph could be used to send messages from one city to another, telegraph lines were needed. Samuel Morse asked the United States Congress to help him build telegraph lines. He asked for thirty thousand dollars to build a line from Washington to Baltimore. He felt sure that business men would be glad to send messages by telegraph and to pay him for his work. Many members of Congress laughed at his idea.

Weeks and weeks went by until it was the last day for the Congress to meet, March 3, 1843. Samuel Morse stayed at the Capitol until ten o'clock in the evening. The Congress still had not voted to give him the money. Morse thought he would have to give up his plan to build the telegraph line. Sadly he went back to his hotel.

The next morning, Miss Annie G. Ellsworth met him

as he was coming down to breakfast. She was the daughter of a friend in Washington. She came forward with a smile, grasped his hand, and said that she had  good news for him. Congress had decided to let him have the money. Congress had voted just a few minutes before midnight. It was the very last thing they had done.

In the spring of 1844, the line was completed. Samuel Morse asked Miss Ellsworth to send the first message. She sent these words from the Bible: *"What hath God wrought!"*

Samuel Morse wrote to his brother Sidney on May 31, 1844: "'<u>What hath God wrought</u>'? Surely none but He who has all hearts in his hands, and turns them as the rivers of water are turned, could so have brought light out of darkness. Sorrow may continue for a night but joy cometh in the morning. Pray for me then, my dear brother, that I may have a heart to praise the Great Deliverer, and in future when discouraged or despairing be enabled to remember His past mercy, and in full faith rest all my cares on him who careth for us."

Communication across a Nation

Messages could now be sent instantly from one part of the country to another. Samuel Morse developed a code to send messages on the telegraph. Dots and dashes were used to represent each letter of the alphabet. The telegraph was changed. Instead of a pencil, it had a metal key which received the messages. The key clicked as it put the code on a paper tape. Telegraph operators quickly learned to send and receive messages using the sound of the clicks.

By 1853, the telegraph was connected to every state east of the Mississippi, except Florida. By 1861, a cable had been laid in the Atlantic Ocean and messages could be sent from America to Europe.

Samuel Morse's dream had come true. Messages could be sent quickly from one place to another.

God would use other men and inventions to make it even easier for people to communicate with one another.

God
bless
America

Alexander Graham Bell

Alexander Graham Bell invented the first telephone. The telegraph could only send coded messages.

With the telephone, people could speak a message over the wire.

Alexander Bell was born in Edinburgh, Scotland, on March 3, 1847. Alexander was one of three sons born to Melville and Eliza Bell. His family and friends called him Aleck.

Alexander's mother taught her sons at home. She taught them grammar, spelling, reading, arithmetic, and art.

Eliza Bell was nearly deaf, but was a good pianist. She taught all three boys to play the piano. Alexander loved music, and played the piano very well. He had a special gift for hearing sounds.

Alexander and his mother were very close. Others spoke to his mother through a special speaking tube. But Alexander learned that if he spoke in very low tones close to her forehead, his mother could understand his words.

Alexander was not given a middle name when he was born. When Alexander was about eleven, a family guest, named Alexander Graham, spent time in their home. Alexander Bell liked Alexander Graham

Communication across a Nation

and decided to take the name Graham for his own middle name. From that time he used the name of Alexander Graham Bell.

Alexander was always curious and tried many experiments. Many of his experiments had to do with sound. He and his brother found that by pressing on their dog's mouth and voice box, they could make the dog sound like he was making words.

Alex's father, Melville Bell, and his grandfather, who was also named Alexander, were both speech teachers. Melville Bell developed a special system of written symbols. The symbols showed exactly how the mouth, tongue, and teeth should be held to make any sound or word. The system was called *visible speech* and could be used for any language. Later it was used to teach the deaf how to speak.

At the age of sixteen, Alexander began to teach others. He first taught music, but later he taught many people the benefits of the *visible speech* method.

When both of Alexander's brothers died of sickness, Melville moved his family to Canada. He thought the climate would be more healthy for his family.

In 1871, Alexander moved to Boston and began teaching at a deaf school. One special student was Mabel Hubbard. Mabel and Alexander grew to love one another and she became his wife in 1877.

During his lifetime, Alexander helped many deaf learn to speak and communicate with their voices. He always had a great love and concern for the deaf and began several schools for the deaf.

Besides teaching the deaf, Alexander Bell was an inventor. Alexander tried to find a way that more than one message could be sent at one time on the telegraph wires. While he was working on this idea, he began to think that it might be possible to send the sound of the human voice over wire.

Alexander wrote the ideas for his inventions in notebooks. His drawing of the earliest telephone does not look like the telephones of today. With the first telephone one person could speak. The person at the other end could only listen to the voice.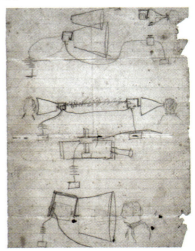

Alexander Graham Bell worked many years to make a telephone that would allow two people to talk to each other.

Alexander Bell needed help with his invention. He hired Thomas Watson to assist him. Thomas Watson knew more about electricity than Bell. He worked with Bell to develop the telephone.

The new invention required a great deal of hard work. Sometimes the inventors were tired and discouraged, but they never gave up.

Bell and Watson tried many experiments. Each time, they wanted to learn something new that would help make the telephone work.

On March 10, 1876, Bell and Watson set up a wire between two rooms. They closed the doors of both rooms. Suddenly, Watson heard Alexander Graham Bell speaking through the telephone, "Mr. Watson, come here. I want you!" That was the first telephone message of history.

At first, people did not think the telephone was an important invention. They could not understand why anyone would need to talk across a wire. Soon,

however, people learned that they could take care of business over the telephone. They learned that they could call to tell others some special news. Finally, many people decided that they wanted a telephone.

Alexander Graham Bell and some other business men set up a telephone company. They began to make telephones and put up wires across the country.

On January 25, 1915, the first telephone call was made from New York to California. Alexander Graham Bell spoke over the telephone in New York. Thomas Watson was in California. And, just as he had done in 1876, Mr. Bell said, "Mr. Watson, come here. I want you!" Mr. Watson answered that it would take him a while to come to New York.

First the telegraph and then the telephone made it possible for people to communicate all the way from the Atlantic Ocean to the Pacific Ocean. News could now travel immediately from coast to coast. People who had gone west were no longer separated from the news from the east.

These inventions opened the way for many other new inventions.

Today, the telegraph and telephone are very different from the inventions of Samuel F. B. Morse and Alexander Graham Bell. They still provide a way for people to communicate with others anywhere in the country and even around the world.

It is important for us to use these inventions to help our nation stay strong. We must remember that God is the one that gives each man the ability to develop new inventions.

148 Chapter 20

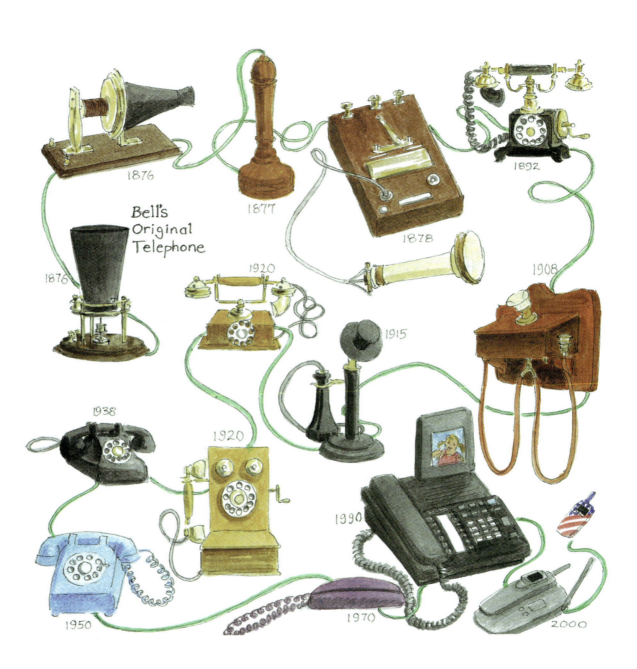

Chapter 21

The Nation Expands

In 1776, when the thirteen colonies declared their independence from England, each state was separate. They each had their own state government.

In 1789, the Constitution was written and accepted by each of the thirteen states. Then there were thirteen states, but only one nation — the United States of America.

Since 1789, many new states have become part of the United States of America. There are now fifty states. Hawaii was the last state to become part of the United States in 1959.

How did the nation expand? The Constitution included a plan for new states to join the United States.

The people of the new territory must wish to be a state. As the people moved west and settled new land, they decided if they wanted to be part of the United States.

When the United States became a nation, the representatives wrote the Constitution and the people agreed to be governed by its laws. When a new territory wanted to be a state, they chose representatives who wrote a Constitution for the state. The people of the territory agreed to be governed by its laws.

The new state Constitution must have the same ideas of liberty and self government which the United States Constitution has. The people of the state must be able to choose representatives who make the laws.

The Congress of the United States includes representatives from each of the states. Each new state must ask the Congress if they can be part of the United States. The Congress must vote to decide

After each of these steps are taken, the territory can become part of the United States of America. Once the new territory is a State, the people choose men or women who will represent them in the Congress of the United States.

These steps help to protect that our nation will continue to be a self governing republic.